Boost Your Self-Esteem

A Comprehensive Guide to Cultivating a Positive Self-Image

Zarekis Silvermist

Copyright 2022. All Rights Reserved.

This document provides exact and reliable information regarding the topic and issues covered. The publication is sold with the idea that the publisheris not required to render accounting, officially permitted, or otherwise qualified services. If advice is necessary, legal or professional, a practiced individual in the profession should be ordered.

From a Declaration of Principles which was accepted and approved equally by a Committee of the American Bar Association and a Committee of Publishers and Associations.

In no way is it legal to reproduce, duplicate, or transmit any part of this document in either electronic means or printed format. Recording of this publication is strictly prohibited, and any storage of this document is not allowed unless with written permission from the publisher. All rights reserved.

The information provided herein is stated to be truthful and consistent. Any liability, in terms of inattention or otherwise, by any usage or abuse of any policies, processes, or Instructions contained within is the solitary and utter responsibility of the recipient reader. Under no circumstances will any legal obligation or blame be held against the publisher for

reparation, damages,or monetary loss due to the information herein, either directly or indirectly. Respective authors own all copyrights not held by the publisher.

The information herein is offered for informational purposes solely and is universal as such. The presentation of the data is without a contract or any guarantee assurance.

Table of content

Chapter 1: Understanding Self-Esteem

- What is self-esteem?

A person's total sense of self-worth and self-value is referred to as their self-esteem, which is a word that describes how they feel about themselves. It is the extent to which a person believes they are capable, deserving of respect, and capable of giving and receiving love. Self-esteem is a mental and emotional state that is generally described as a positive self-regard and a belief in one's talents and potential. This belief in one's own abilities and potential is what gives rise to self-esteem.

The concept of self-esteem is basic to human psychology and plays an important part in both our day-to-day happiness and our ability to achieve our goals. When we have a healthy sense of self-worth, we are more likely to experience feelings of self-assurance and competence, which can pave the way for increased levels of happiness, success, and fulfillment in our lives. When our self-esteem is low, we may struggle with feelings of inadequacy, self-doubt, and low self-worth, all of which can negatively impact our mental health, relationships, and overall quality of life. On the other hand, when our self-esteem is high, we may struggle with these feelings less frequently.

The way we were raised, the experiences we've had in life, the culture we come from, and the beliefs we hold personally are all elements that might have an impact on our sense of self-worth. For instance, those who were raised in households that were overly critical or negligent may struggle with low self-esteem as a result of internalizing the negative messages that were sent to them during their childhood. In a similar vein, those who have been victims of trauma or discrimination may also battle with low self-esteem as a result of the effect that these experiences have had on their perception of their own value.

There are a number of distinct schools of thought that have been put forth in an effort to explain the fundamentals of self-esteem and how it evolves over time. The idea that our level of self-esteem is determined by our sense of competence and achievement in numerous facets of life, such as work, relationships, and hobbies, is one of the more prevalent schools of thought. According to this notion, our sense of self-worth increases when we have instances in which we feel successful and accomplished in the aforementioned domains; conversely, our sense of self-worth might diminish when we experience instances of failure or setbacks.

According to a second school of thought, our social contacts and the feedback we get from other people are major contributors to our sense of self-worth. According to this theory, we have a propensity to depend our sense of self-worth on how other people view us and the degree to which they regard us as unique individuals. Therefore, receiving positive feedback and validation from others has the potential to increase our self-esteem, while receiving negative feedback or rejection has the potential to diminish it.

It is evident that maintaining a good level of self-esteem is necessary for our overall well-being as well as the success we have in life, and this is true regardless of the specific elements that have an effect on our self-esteem. A healthy degree of self-esteem enables us to pursue our goals and objectives with confidence, to create meaningful connections with other people, and to cope with the challenges and disappointments that will surely present themselves to us throughout our lives. On the other hand, having a poor self-esteem can be detrimental to our progress and prevent us from reaching our full potential, which can result in feelings of despondency, worry, and hopelessness.

We are fortunate to have access to a wide variety of methods that can assist us in enhancing our self-esteem and developing a more favorable view of ourselves. These tactics may include learning to confront negative self-talk and replacing it with messages that are more positive and affirming, practicing self-care and self-compassion, creating and attaining goals that are achievable, and developing good connections with other people. We may realize our full potential and live our lives to the very fullest extent if we take the necessary efforts to boost our self-esteem.

- Why is self-esteem important?

The mental and emotional health of an individual is significantly impacted by their level of self-esteem. It is a measure of a person's overall estimation of their own value and worth as a human being. It is absolutely necessary, in order to live a life that is both rewarding and satisfying, to maintain a healthy degree of self-esteem.

It's crucial to have high self-esteem for a number of reasons, but one of the most important is that it affects how we view ourselves and our capabilities. People who are confident in themselves and their abilities are more likely to have a favorable self-image and to have faith that they can accomplish what they set out to do. They are more willing to put themselves out there and try new things, even if they don't succeed at them at first. This is due to the fact that they have a robust feeling of their own value and are not readily deterred by failures or obstructions in their path.

People who have poor self-esteem, on the other hand, have a tendency to have a negative opinion of themselves and may have doubts about their talents. They could have feelings of inadequacy or inferiority to those around them, which makes them reluctant to take on new challenges. This can start a vicious cycle of self-doubt and insecurity, which can have a substantial negative effect on a person's mental health as well as their overall well-being.

The way in which we relate to other people is also impacted by our level of self-esteem, in addition to the way in which we view ourselves. People who have a healthy sense of their own worth are more likely to have positive interactions with others and to communicate in a more confident and forthright manner. Additionally, they are more likely to establish healthy boundaries and to advocate for themselves when it is required.

On the other hand, those who have poor self-esteem are more likely to struggle with social anxiety and find it difficult to assert themselves when they are in relationships with others. They may be more easily swayed by the influence of their peers and have a more difficult time refusing the requests or demands of other people.

The way we feel about ourselves might also have an effect on our physical wellbeing. Researchers have found that people who have higher levels of self-esteem tend to have better overall health outcomes. These include lower rates of melancholy and anxiety, enhanced immune function, and a reduced chance of developing chronic diseases such as heart disease and diabetes.

In conclusion, maintaining a healthy degree of self-esteem is absolutely necessary in order to find happiness and fulfillment in one's life. When we have a healthy sense of self-esteem and confidence in our capabilities, we are more likely to follow our interests and pursue our hobbies. We are also more inclined to engage in activities that bring us joy and satisfaction, which can have a favorable impact on our mental and emotional well-being. When we are happy, we are more likely to engage in things that provide us joy and fulfillment.

In conclusion, having a healthy sense of self-worth is essential to the mental and emotional well of an individual. It has an effect on how we view ourselves and our capabilities, it has an effect on the connections we have with other people, and it can even have an effect on our physical health. We may lead lives that are more meaningful and enjoyable, accomplish our goals, and create relationships with ourselves and others that are healthier if we make it a priority to concentrate on improving our self-esteem.

- The consequences of low self-esteem

A lack of self-esteem can have a wide range of unfavorable effects on an individual's life, including adverse effects on their mental and emotional health, their relationships, and their quality of life in general. When we have low self-esteem, we may struggle with feelings of inadequacy, self-doubt, and low self-worth, all of which can lead to a number of unfavorable outcomes. When we have low self-esteem, others may treat us differently.

A detrimental effect that poor self-esteem can have on our mental health is one of the most severe repercussions of the condition. Individuals who have a poor self-esteem may have a harder time coping with the challenges and demands of day-to-day living, which may make them more susceptible to a variety of mental health conditions, including depression, anxiety, and others. Low self-esteem can also result in negative thought patterns and self-talk, both of which can further exacerbate the aforementioned mental health problems and make it more challenging to overcome them.

A lack of respect for oneself can also have a significant influence on the connections we have with other people. People who have poor self-esteem may find it difficult to build healthy, pleasant connections with others because they may believe that they are not deserving of love and affection from others around them. They may also be more prone to tolerate negative or abusive behavior from others since they may feel that they do not deserve better. This could be because they believe that they do not deserve better. In addition, having low self-esteem can result in feelings of envy, animosity, and jealousy toward other people who are seen as being more successful or attractive, which further strains interpersonal connections.

Low self-esteem has a number of negative effects, one of which is that it can restrict our potential and prevent us from achieving our objectives and pursuing our aspirations. People who have poor self-esteem are more prone to avoid taking risks and putting themselves in difficult situations because they are afraid of failing or being rejected. This can result in lost opportunities for personal and professional development, as well as a sensation of being stuck in a rut and lacking fulfillment in one's life.

A lack of respect for oneself can also have an effect on our physical wellbeing. Researchers have found that those who have poor levels of self-esteem have a greater propensity to participate in dangerous activities, such as abusing drugs and alcohol, engaging in unsafe sexual practices, and other unhealthy habits. These practices may have severe repercussions not only for our physical health but also for our mental and emotional well-being as well.

Overall, having poor self-esteem has repercussions that are far-reaching and can have a significant influence on our life. These repercussions can be substantial. Nevertheless, it is essential to keep in mind that there are methods at our disposal that can assist us in enhancing our self-esteem and developing a more favorable view of ourselves. We can start to overcome the negative consequences of low self-esteem and unleash our full potential if we learn to confront negative self-talk, engage in self-care behaviors such as practicing self-compassion and engaging in self-care activities, and create good relationships with others.

Chapter 2: Identifying the Source of Low Self-Esteem

- Childhood experiences and self-esteem

Experiences that occur during a person's formative years can have a substantial influence on the individual's sense of self-worth. The views that children have about themselves and their value as individuals can be influenced by the manner in which they are treated as youngsters as well as the messages they hear during their formative years. Having a good sense of self-esteem can be fostered by positive experiences, whereas having low self-esteem and a poor picture of oneself can be the result of having terrible experiences.

The quality of a child's connections with the adults who care for them is one of the most influential aspects in the formation of that child's sense of self-worth. It is more likely for children to acquire a good sense of self-esteem if they get love, affection, and support from their primary caregivers, such as their parents or other key caregivers. They get the sense that kids are cherished and respected, and as a result, they learn to trust other people. On the other side, children who are subjected to neglect, abuse, or other forms of maltreatment may struggle with poor self-esteem and feelings of worthlessness or shame. This is because these children are more likely to internalize these negative emotions. Later in life, they could also have trouble trusting others and maintaining healthy relationships due to their past experiences.

The messages that children acquire about their capabilities and worth as people are an additional significant aspect in childhood experiences and the development of healthy self-esteem in adults. Children are more likely to cultivate a healthy self-image and a robust feeling of self-worth if they are complimented on their efforts and achievements throughout their formative years. They gain the ability to have faith in their own capabilities and to feel pride in the things they have accomplished. On the other hand, children who are constantly chastised or put down may develop poor self-esteem, leading them to believe that they are not good enough or that their efforts are pointless.

A child's sense of self-worth can also be significantly influenced by the relationships they have with their peers. Children who have positive social experiences with their peers, such as making friends and feeling accepted, have a greater chance of developing a healthy sense of self-esteem than children who do not have these kind of experiences. They have the sense that they are valued by others and that they belong to a group. On the other hand, children who are bullied, rejected, or socially isolated may suffer with feelings of inadequacy or self-doubt and may develop poor self-esteem as a result of these negative life experiences.

Last but not least, the experiences that children encounter while they are in school can also have an effect on their sense of self-worth. Children are more likely to cultivate a healthy self-image and a robust feeling of self-worth if they are given good feedback from their teachers and if they have the perception that they are successful academically. They have the conviction that they can do what they set out to do and are aware that their skills are highly regarded. In contrast, children who have academic difficulties or who receive unfavorable comments from their professors are more likely to develop low self-esteem and the belief that they are neither intelligent nor capable.

In conclusion, the events that occur during a person's upbringing can have a substantial effect on the individual's sense of self-worth. A good sense of self-esteem can be developed by the cultivation of positive experiences such as loving connections with caregivers, receiving praise and encouragement for accomplishments, cultivating positive peer relationships, and achieving success in academic endeavors. A lack of self-esteem and a poor picture of oneself might be the result of having gone through challenging times, such as being mistreated, receiving criticism or rejection, or having academic difficulties. Parents, caregivers, and educators can work to create positive environments for children that promote healthy self-esteem and a positive sense of self-worth for children by understanding the impact of childhood experiences on self-esteem. These environments can be created by understanding the impact of childhood experiences on self-esteem.

- Negative self-talk and its effects

Negative self-talk is a frequent yet dangerous behavior that can have a significant influence on both our mental and emotional health. This habit can have a significant impact on our mental and emotional health. The term "negative self-talk" refers to the critical, self-deprecating, or judgemental ideas that we have about ourselves during our inner conversation or during the thoughts that we have about ourselves. This kind of thinking can be damaging because it tends to perpetuate negative attitudes about ourselves. These beliefs, in turn, can contribute to feelings of inadequacy, low self-esteem, and even depression.

The impacts of negative self-talk can be far-reaching and can have an effect on many aspects of our lives, such as the relationships we have, the jobs we do, and our overall sense of well-being. A prominent effect of negative self-talk is that it can add to emotions of anxiety and stress, which is one of the most significant repercussions. Negative self-talk is when we tell ourselves that we are not good enough, smart enough, or capable enough, which can lead to feelings of self-doubt and uncertainty. When we engage in negative self-talk, we are essentially telling ourselves that we are not good enough, smart enough, or capable enough. These feelings can then rise to anxiety and tension when we worry about our ability to handle specific situations or tasks. This is because we doubt our ability to control the situation or activity at hand.

Our connections with other people can be negatively impacted when we engage in negative self-talk. When we engage in negative self-talk, we increase the likelihood that we will project those negative views onto other people and make the assumption that others share our poor perspective of ourselves. Because of this, we may come to believe that we are unworthy of love or affection, which can make it difficult for us to develop trusting and intimate connections with others. Furthermore, negative self-talk can lead to sentiments of jealously and resentment toward other people, particularly those who are viewed as being more successful or attractive. This can further damage relationships.

One more thing that might happen as a result of negative self-talk is that it can restrict our potential and impede us from achieving our objectives and pursuing our aspirations. We may be more prone to avoid difficulties and take risks when we engage in negative self-talk because we fear failing at the task at hand or being rejected by others. This can result in lost opportunities for personal and professional development, as well as a sensation of being stuck in a rut and lacking fulfillment in one's life.

Our negative internal dialogue can also have an effect on our physical well-being. Research has indicated that having a critical dialogue with oneself might lead to stress-related disorders such as cardiovascular disease, high blood pressure, and chronic pain. Negative self-talk can also lead to poor self-care practices, such as overeating or not exercising enough, both of which can make existing health problems even worse.

The impacts of negative self-talk can be widespread and can have an effect on a variety of facets of our lives. However, it is essential to keep in mind that we have the ability to alter the way in which we talk to ourselves and build a more favorable image of ourselves. We can begin to overcome the harmful consequences of negative self-talk and unleash our full potential if we learn to recognize and question negative self-talk, engage in self-care and self-compassion practices, and cultivate good connections with others.

- The influence of social media on self-esteem

The use of social media has become an integral part of contemporary life, and as a result, it has had a considerable influence on a variety of facets of our lives, including the way we feel about ourselves. Users of social media platforms such as Facebook, Instagram, and Twitter have access to a never-ending stream of information about their friends, family members, and other people they know. Even though using social media can be a helpful tool for maintaining connections with others, it also has the potential to have a detrimental impact on our sense of self-worth.

The principal manner in which the use of social media might affect our sense of self-worth is by leading us to set goals for ourselves that are impossible to achieve. The lives of other people are often presented on social media in a way that has been carefully edited to highlight only the most upbeat and interesting aspects of their life. This can lead to a sense of pressure to project a similarly ideal image of ourselves online, which, if we are unable to live up to these expectations, can lead to feelings of inadequacy and self-doubt.

Comparisons with other people are yet another manner in which our self-esteem can be negatively impacted by social media. When we view pictures on social media of other people's lives that appear to be wonderful, we may experience feelings of envy or insecurity about our own lives. This can cause us to compare ourselves to others and come to the conclusion that we are not as good as they are, which can lead to us having negative views about ourselves and our own value.

Because it makes us more vulnerable to cyberbullying and other forms of online abuse, using social media can also have a detrimental effect on our sense of self-worth. Negative comments or messages can be upsetting and destructive to our self-esteem, particularly if they are directed at our looks or other areas of our identity. This is especially true when the subject of the comment or message is our appearance.

On the other hand, the use of social media platforms can also have a beneficial effect on our sense of self-worth. For instance, social media can serve as a forum for self-expression and creative endeavors, giving us the opportunity to exhibit both our abilities and our passions. Because technology allows us to connect with others who share our experiences and interests, it also has the potential to provide us a sense of community and to be a source of support.

In spite of these prospective advantages, it is essential to be conscious of the ways in which the use of social media might affect our sense of self-worth and to take actions to limit the negative consequences of these influences. If we are battling with feelings of poor self-esteem or inadequacy, this may entail reducing the amount of time we spend on social media, being conscious of the sorts of content we consume and share online, and reaching out for support from friends or a mental health professional.

In conclusion, it can be said that the use of social media has had a substantial impact, both positively and negatively, on our sense of self-worth. The use of social media can be a helpful tool for maintaining connections with others and expressing ourselves, but it also has the potential to lead to the formation of unrealistic expectations, the encouragement of unhealthy social comparisons, and the risk of being subjected to cyberbullying and other forms of online harassment. We can make good and healthy use of social media by being cognizant of the ways in which it might damage our self-esteem and by taking precautions to preserve our mental health. This will allow us to use social media in a way that is beneficial and healthy.

Chapter 3: Strategies for Building Self-Esteem

- Cultivating a positive mindset

A important component of one's personal development and overall health is the cultivation of a positive mental attitude. The way we think and feel about ourselves, other people, and the world that surrounds us is what is meant by the term "positive attitude." Instead of focussing on the unpleasant parts of our lives and experiences, it involves concentrating on the more good aspects of those things. The cultivation of a positive mentality can result in a wide variety of good outcomes, such as increased enjoyment, enhanced relationships, and higher resilience in the face of adversity.

Developing an attitude of appreciation is a good place to start when you want to cultivate a more upbeat and optimistic outlook on life. Being grateful is centering one's attention on the favorable aspects of one's life and voicing appreciation for such things. This can be as straightforward as setting aside a few minutes every day to think on the things for which we are grateful, such as our health, the relationships we have, or the things we have accomplished. According to a number of studies, cultivating an attitude of thankfulness can result in enhanced levels of happiness and well-being, in addition to improvements in one's physical health.

The cultivation of a good mindset requires a number of fundamental practices, one of which is the development of self-compassion. Self-compassion refers to the practice of approaching one's own actions with kindness and understanding, rather than judgment and criticism. This requires us to recognize our shortcomings and blunders without condemning or berating ourselves for them. Self-compassion increases our likelihood of feeling confident and capable, which in turn can lead to higher resilience when confronted with adversity.

In order to cultivate a positive mindset, one of the most important things we can do is to shift our attention away from our shortcomings and missed opportunities and toward our successes instead. This entails taking the time to recognize and rejoice in our accomplishments rather than obsessing on our failings and failings we have yet to do. When we concentrate on the positive aspects of our lives, such as our achievements and capabilities, we are more likely to experience feelings of self-assurance and competence, which, in turn, can help us achieve greater levels of success and satisfaction in our lives.

Additionally, surrounding ourselves with good influences is an important part of developing a healthy mental attitude. This entails pursuing connections and experiences that are pleasant and uplifting, rather than ones that are negative and draining, in order to achieve this goal. When we surround ourselves with good influences, we increase the likelihood that we will experience happiness and fulfillment, which in turn can lead to increased levels of success and well-being.

The last step in developing a more optimistic outlook is to develop a mindfulness practice. Instead of allowing ourselves to become distracted or concerned, practicing mindfulness requires us to completely engage in the activities and sensations that we are having in the here and now. When we engage in mindful practices, we increase the likelihood that we will experience a sense of being grounded and centered, which in turn can assist us in managing negative emotions such as stress and worry.

In conclusion, developing a more optimistic frame of mind is one of the most important aspects of one's overall growth and health. We can begin to shift our mindset toward a more positive and fulfilling outlook on life by engaging in mindfulness practices such as gratitude, self-compassion, focusing on our strengths and accomplishments, surrounding ourselves with positive influences, and focusing on our strengths and accomplishments.

- Self-care and self-compassion

To keep one's mental and emotional health in good standing, it is necessary to practice both self-care and self-compassion on a regular basis. Self-compassion is the practice of extending kindness, understanding, and support to oneself in times of difficulty or distress. While self-care refers to the actions we take to care for ourselves physically, emotionally, and spiritually, self-compassion involves extending these same things to oneself. These techniques, when combined, have the potential to help us become more resilient, establish a good view of ourselves, and improve our general well-being.

Practicing good self-care is making a conscious effort to meet our physiological, psychological, and spiritual requirements in a holistic manner. This might include things like obtaining regular exercise, maintaining a nutritious diet, getting a enough amount of sleep, spending time in nature, and participating in activities that offer us pleasure or help us relax. When it comes to self-care, there is no one-size-fits-all strategy, and what is effective for one individual may not be effective for another. The most important thing is to give careful consideration to the steps we take to care for ourselves and to put our own health and happiness first.

On the other side, practicing self-compassion is treating oneself with the same degree of empathy, understanding, and support that we would offer to a close friend or loved one. This requires us to recognize our own anguish and challenges without passing judgment or offering criticism, as well as to show compassion and understanding toward ourselves in the same way that we would show it to others. Recognizing that we are all human and that it is natural to endure suffering, struggle, and obstacles in life is an essential component in practicing self-compassion.

Self-compassion and self-care are two separate practices that, when combined, can help us become more resilient and improve our overall well-being. We can cultivate a positive self-image, increase our self-esteem, and reduce feelings of stress, anxiety, and depression if we consciously take actions to care for ourselves and if we extend compassion and understanding to ourselves in times of difficulty. These actions can be done in conjunction with one another.

Self-care and self-compassion can be practiced in a variety of ways, and it is essential for each of us to determine the methods that are most effective for us as unique individuals. The following are some practices that are examples of self-care:

- Maintaining a regular exercise routine or engaging in other forms of physical activity - Eating a nutritious and well-balanced diet - Obtaining an adequate amount of sleep and rest - Spending time in nature or participating in other forms of outdoor activity
- Participating in things that bring us joy or relaxation, such as hobbies or pastimes; - Spending time with loved ones or participating in other social activities; - Practicing relaxation techniques, such as meditation or deep breathing

The following are some practices that are examples of self-compassion:

- Speaking nice things to oneself or words of encouragement
- Recognizing that we are all human and that it is natural for us to endure sorrow and struggle - Admitting our own suffering and challenges without passing judgment or offering criticism - Doing so without judging or criticizing others
- Extending the same level of compassion and understanding to ourselves that we would to a close friend or loved one

In conclusion, the practices of self-care and self-compassion are crucial components of a healthy lifestyle for the mind and the emotions. We may nurture a good self-image, build resilience, and improve our general well-being by taking conscious efforts to care for ourselves and by giving love, understanding, and support to ourselves in times of adversity. If we make our own health and happiness a top priority and show compassion and care for ourselves, we will be able to lead lives that are more rewarding and enjoyable.

- Setting realistic goals and achieving them

It is crucial to one's personal growth and achievement to establish attainable goals and then work toward their accomplishment. Setting goals not only helps us to concentrate our efforts, but also gives our lives a sense of direction and purpose. However, in order for us to be successful in accomplishing our objectives, we need to make sure that the goals we establish are not only reasonable and doable, but also in line with the capabilities and resources we possess.

Finding out what our values and top priorities are should be one of the first things we do when we start the process of defining objectives that are realistic. This requires us to give some thought to the things that are significant to us and the goals that we have for our lives. As soon as we have a distinct understanding of our core beliefs and priorities, we can move on to the process of establishing objectives for ourselves that are congruent with our beliefs and that will assist us in achieving the outcomes we have in mind.

Additionally, it is essential to formulate objectives that are particular and quantifiable. This entails framing our objectives in explicit language and determining the measures by which we will judge our level of achievement. For instance, if our objective is to enhance our level of physical fitness, we can decide to establish a certain target for reducing our body fat percentage or for jogging a given distance within a predetermined amount of time. Because we have clearly defined and measurable objectives, we are able to monitor our progress and make course corrections as required to ensure that we remain on track.

The process of defining objectives that are realistic also involves the essential step of breaking those goals down into smaller, more attainable tasks. This requires us to first determine the particular steps that need to be taken in order for us to attain our goals, and then to break those activities down into more manageable and granular responsibilities. This can help our objectives feel less overwhelming and more attainable, which in turn can help us keep motivated and on track with our progress toward achieving them.

Setting goals that are difficult to achieve but not insurmountable is another essential step in the process. When setting goals, it's important to strike a balance between how challenging they are and how manageable they are. If the goals are too demanding, it can be depressing and lead to emotions of failure and dissatisfaction. We may push our limits and foster personal growth by establishing goals that are difficult but not insurmountable, and in doing so, we can keep our sense of momentum and drive intact.

In conclusion, it is essential that we acknowledge and appreciate our accomplishments as well as draw wisdom from our mistakes. After reaching our objectives, we may feel a sense of accomplishment and satisfaction; but, it is essential to take some time to evaluate what aspects of our efforts were successful and which were not, and to adapt our strategies accordingly for our subsequent objectives. We may continue to develop and get better over time if we recognize and appreciate our achievements and draw wisdom from our setbacks.

In conclusion, one of the most important aspects of personal development and success is the ability to successfully create and accomplish one's goals. We can accomplish our goals and live lives that are more fulfilling and satisfying if we first determine our values and priorities, then write down our objectives in a way that is specific and measurable, then break those objectives down into more manageable steps, then establish targets that are challenging but doable, and finally, celebrate and learn from our successes along the way.

- Overcoming perfectionism and fear of failure

Both perfectionism and the fear of failing at anything are widespread problems that can have a considerable negative effect on our mental and emotional well-being. To be a perfectionist means to hold oneself to an exceedingly high standard and to make it a goal of one's life to achieve perfection in every facet of one's existence. On the other side, the fear of failing is characterized by an irrational dread of either committing errors or falling short of one's objectives. These problems can make us feel stressed out, anxious, and full of self-doubt, and they can impede us from realizing our full potential.

Recognizing the effect that difficulties like as perfectionism and the fear of failing have on our lives is one of the first things that must be done in order to make progress toward overcoming these problems. It is possible that we are suffering with perfectionism and the fear of failing without even being aware of the fact that we are having these problems. We can start to notice the ways in which perfectionism and the fear of failing are hurting our lives if we take the time to reflect on our thoughts and behaviors and give ourselves permission to do so.

To overcome perfectionism and the fear of failing, reframing our thinking about these problems is an additional significant step that must be taken. It is possible to reframe our perception of mistakes and setbacks so that we see them not as evidence of our inadequacies but as opportunities for personal development and advancement. We can begin to approach issues with a sense of curiosity and openness rather than a sense of fear and worry if we reframe our thinking in this way and look at them in this way.

In addition to being a crucial component of overcoming perfectionism and the fear of failing, the practice of self-compassion is also vital. We have the ability to learn to be kinder and more understanding toward ourselves when we make errors or fall short of our goals. Rather than being hard on ourselves when we do this, we can learn to practice self-compassion. It is possible for us to remind ourselves that it is normal for us to make errors and that our value as individuals is not dependent on the accomplishments or successes we have had.

In addition, it is essential that we provide ourselves with goals that are attainable and that we acknowledge and appreciate our accomplishments, regardless of how minor they may be. Building our confidence and self-esteem can help us combat the detrimental effects of perfectionism and fear of failure. This can be accomplished by establishing objectives that are within our reach and giving ourselves credit for accomplishing those goals.

The final step in overcoming perfectionism and the fear of failing is to seek help from other people. This can be a vital part of the process. This can be accomplished by having a conversation with a dependable friend or member of the family, consulting with a mental health expert for help, or signing up for a support group. We might feel less alone and more supported in our efforts to overcome perfectionism and fear of failure if we connect with other people who understand our issues and can relate to the challenges we face.

In conclusion, overcoming perfectionism and the fear of failing is a process that is never finished; it requires self-reflection, self-compassion, and a willingness to rethink our thinking about the issues at hand. We can learn to approach obstacles with an attitude of openness and curiosity rather than fear and worry if we learn to create objectives that are achievable, celebrate our victories, and seek assistance from others. These are the steps that will help us grow our confidence and self-esteem. We can overcome perfectionism and the fear of failing if we put in the time and effort, and this will allow us to lead lives that are more rewarding and enjoyable.

Chapter 4: Maintaining High Self-Esteem

- Dealing with setbacks and failures

Confronting and learning from one's mistakes is a crucial component of both personal development and professional achievement. Even though having setbacks and failing at anything can be challenging and disheartening, they also present an opportunity for personal development and growth. We can learn to deal with negative experiences, such as setbacks and disappointments, in a way that is useful and constructive if we cultivate a positive mentality and employ effective coping mechanisms.

Acknowledging and accepting one's mistakes and misfortunes is a crucial first step in the process of overcoming obstacles and falling short of one's goals. This implies acknowledging that mistakes and setbacks are an inevitable part of the process of learning and maturing, and that these experiences do not constitute a reflection of who we are or the capabilities we possess. We may prevent ourselves from becoming mired in a pessimistic frame of mind and can instead start to concentrate on moving forward by acknowledging that mistakes and other kinds of setbacks are a natural and expected part of the process.

It is also essential that we gain wisdom from our mistakes and other forms of defeat. This requires us to take stock of what went wrong, what we may have done differently, and what we can take away from the experience as a whole. By stepping back from the situation and approaching it with an objective point of view, we can get useful insights that will assist us in improving and expanding in the years to come.

Having self-compassion is another crucial step in the right direction when it comes to overcoming obstacles and falling short of goals. This involves having a compassionate and understanding attitude toward ourselves rather than one that is judgmental and critical. When we face obstacles and fall short of our goals, we run the risk of beating ourselves up or coming to believe that we are not deserving of success. However, engaging in self-compassion practices can assist us in approaching the circumstance with a more constructive and optimistic frame of mind, as well as in bouncing back from setbacks in a more timely manner.

When coping with setbacks and disappointments, seeking assistance from other people is another essential step to take. This implies seeking emotional support, advice, or direction from friends, family, or coworkers, and reaching out to them for help. When we open up about our past experiences to others, we not only give them the opportunity to learn from them but also receive vital input that can assist us in moving ahead.

In conclusion, it is essential to maintain our drive and concentration on our objectives, even when we encounter obstacles and experiences failure. Instead of obsessing on the past or being concerned about the future, we should keep a positive mindset and concentrate on the aspects of our situation over which we have some measure of control. Even in the face of challenges, we are able to keep moving forward and making progress if we maintain our motivation and keep our attention fixed on our objectives.

In conclusion, overcoming obstacles and falling short of one's goals is a crucial component of both personal development and professional achievement. We can learn to deal with setbacks and failures in a constructive and positive manner, and we can continue to grow and improve over time if we do the following: recognize and accept setbacks and failures; learn from our experiences; practice self-compassion; seek support from others; and stay motivated and focused on our goals.

- Avoiding comparison traps

In this day and age, it is quite simple to get caught up in the comparison game. Images of people who appear to have everything, including beautiful bodies, perfect relationships, and perfect occupations, are continually presented to us by many forms of media, including social media, advertising, and other forms of media. This can cause us to evaluate ourselves in relation to others, leading to feelings of inadequacy or unworthiness. Nevertheless, it is essential that we acknowledge the detrimental effect that comparison can have on our mental and emotional well-being and that we take active measures to prevent ourselves from slipping into the comparison trap.

Recognizing the detrimental effect that comparing oneself to others may have on one's sense of self-worth and general well-being is one of the first things that must be done in order to avoid falling into the trap of comparison. When we compare ourselves to other people, we frequently concentrate on the positive qualities and achievements of those other people, while dismissing our own. This can give rise to feelings of inadequacy, self-doubt, and low self-esteem, all of which have the potential to have a detrimental effect on our mental and emotional health.

Concentrating on one's own virtues and achievements is an additional necessary step in escaping the allure of the comparison trap. We don't need to judge ourselves by the standards of others; rather, we should concentrate on our own successes and the ways in which our lives have improved. Building our confidence and self-esteem can help us combat the damaging effects of comparison, and celebrating our own accomplishments and recognizing our own qualities is a great way to do so.

In addition to this, it is essential to put some thought into the things that we read and watch, as well as the people that we associate with. It can be challenging to resist being caught up in the comparison trap if we are continually confronted with pictures and messages that lead us to believe that we are not good enough or deserving of respect. We may limit the likelihood of being exposed to negative messages that cause feelings of comparison and inadequacy by being careful of the media we consume and the people with whom we spend our time.

Keeping a compassionate attitude toward oneself is another essential step in escaping the allure of destructive comparison. We have the ability to learn to be kinder and more understanding toward ourselves when we make errors or fall short of our goals. Rather than being hard on ourselves when we do this, we can learn to practice self-compassion. It is possible for us to remind ourselves that it is normal for us to make errors and that our value as individuals is not dependent on the accomplishments or successes we have had.

Last but not least, reaching out to other people for support can be an effective strategy for escaping the comparison trap. This can be accomplished by having a conversation with a dependable friend or member of the family, consulting with a mental health expert for help, or signing up for a support group. We can feel less alone and more supported in our efforts to avoid falling into the comparison trap if we connect with other people who understand our challenges and share those struggles.

To summarize, avoiding falling into the comparison trap is an ongoing exercise that calls for self-reflection, self-compassion, and a desire to concentrate on one's own positive qualities and achievements. We may lessen the detrimental effects of comparison on ourselves and enhance our self-esteem and confidence if we are careful of the media we take in and the people we associate with, if we engage in self-compassion, and if we look to others for assistance. We can lead lives that are more full and enjoyable if we take the time and effort to avoid falling into the comparison trap.

- Mindfulness and self-awareness

Both mindfulness and self-awareness are significant concepts that can have a significant bearing on the development and well-being of the individual practicing them. The ability to identify and make sense of one's own thoughts, feelings, and actions is referred to as self-awareness. Mindfulness is the practice of being present in the moment and completely engaged with our experiences, while self-awareness refers to the ability to do so.

One of the primary advantages of practicing mindfulness and increasing our level of self-awareness is that doing so can assist us in being better able to control our feelings and responses. We are able to better regulate our sentiments and respond in a way that is more constructive and beneficial if we are more present in the moment and conscious of our thoughts and feelings. This has the potential to assist us in lowering our levels of stress and anxiety, enhancing the quality of our interactions with other people, and boosting our general well-being.

Another advantage of practicing mindfulness and self-awareness is that they can assist us in recognizing and challenging unhelpful thinking patterns and beliefs, which is a benefit in and of itself. We can learn to realize when we are indulging in negative self-talk or activities that are self-destructive if we cultivate a greater awareness of our thoughts and feelings. This has the potential to assist us in challenging these destructive patterns and replacing them with ones that are more constructive and positive.

Both mindfulness and self-awareness have the potential to assist us in developing closer connections with others around us. When we communicate with other people, we can demonstrate greater awareness and attentiveness to the requirements and feelings of other people if we are more present in such encounters. This can allow us to develop relationships that are not just stronger but also more meaningful, and it can also help us interact with people more effectively.

In addition, practicing mindfulness and increasing our awareness of ourselves might assist us in becoming better decision-makers. We are better able to examine our options and come to decisions that are in line with our values and goals if we are more present in the moment and mindful of our own thoughts and emotions. This has the potential to assist us in achieving our objectives and leading a life that is more rewarding and gratifying.

It is essential to engage in consistent practice if one wishes to develop their capacity for mindfulness and self-awareness. This could involve activities such as meditation or journaling, or it could be as simple as setting aside some time each day to think about and write down our emotions and thoughts. We may start to cultivate a better feeling of presence and awareness in our day-to-day lives if we incorporate mindfulness and self-awareness practices on a consistent basis into our daily routines.

In conclusion, mindfulness and self-awareness are two essential concepts that have the potential to have a significant influence on the development and well-being of an individual. We may better manage our emotions and reactions, uncover and confront harmful thinking patterns and beliefs, enhance our relationships with others, and make better decisions that are in alignment with our values and goals if we practice mindfulness and self-awareness. We may create a better feeling of present and awareness in our day-to-day lives by making mindfulness and self-awareness regular parts of our routines. This will allow us to lead lives that are more meaningful and rewarding overall.

- Continuing your journey of self-improvement

The process of continuing on the path of self-improvement is an ongoing one that calls for devotion, effort, and a willingness to develop and adapt. It requires taking an active role in both our personal and professional growth, as well as committing to an ongoing process of self-improvement through the acquisition of new knowledge and skills. You can continue your quest toward self-improvement by following these suggestions:

1. Establish Your Goals In order to continue on your path to self-improvement, one of the most important things you can do is establish goals that are both clear and explicit. You can determine the aspects of your life in which you would like to see an improvement by defining objectives and developing a plan for how you intend to achieve those goals. Check that your objectives are

attainable, quantifiable, and practical, and make sure you have a strategy in place to accomplish all of these things.

2. Make education a priority Learning is a process that continues throughout one's life, and it is necessary for both personal and professional development. Make a steadfast commitment to consistently enhancing your skill set and expanding your knowledge base. This can be accomplished through traditional schooling, participation in online courses, or even the simple act of reading books and articles. If you make education a top priority, you will be able to keep up with the most

recent developments and industry standards in your profession, as well as develop new abilities that will assist you in reaching the goals you have set for yourself.

3. Engage in Regular Self-Reflection

Engaging in regular self-reflection is an important component of both personal growth and development. Spend some time thinking about your ideas, actions, and behaviors, and pinpoint the areas in which you feel you can make improvements. This can be accomplished through the practice of journaling, meditation, or simply setting aside a few minutes each day to reflect on your activities and the feelings they evoke.

4. Ask for Feedback Getting feedback from other people is an important part of the process of growing as an individual and developing one's potential. Request input from coworkers, friends, and family members, and be willing to consider criticism, even if it's not favorable. Make use of this feedback to help you find areas in which you have room for improvement, and then commit to making adjustments and developing yourself as a person.

5. Create a Support System One of the most important things you can do to continue on your path to self-improvement is to create a support system that includes your family, friends, and coworkers. Put yourself in the company of people who will encourage and uplift you, as well as those who are fully invested in your progress and advancement. Make effective use of this support system so that it can assist you in remaining motivated and focused on achieving your goals.

6. Make Self-Care a Priority One of the most important things you can do to continue making progress on your path

to bettering yourself is to make it a priority to care for your physical, emotional, and mental health. Check that you are receiving enough sleep, that you are eating well, and that you are regularly engaging in physical activity. Make time in your schedule to engage in things that offer you joy and relaxation, and practice relaxation techniques like meditation or deep breathing to help lessen the effects of stress and anxiety.

In conclusion, continuing your road toward self-improvement is a continual process that takes dedication, effort, and a commitment to growing and changing in the future. You may continue to grow and develop as an individual while also achieving your personal and professional goals if you create goals, make learning a top priority, engage in self-reflection, seek feedback, construct a support system, and practice self-care. You can become the most successful and happy version of yourself if you put in the time and effort to cultivate a life that is fulfilling and satisfying.

www.ingramcontent.com/pod-product-compliance
Ingram Content Group UK Ltd.
Pitfield, Milton Keynes, MK11 3LW, UK
UKHW020139250726
13967UKWH00002B/749

9 781088 202982